Mr Steggels
Selective Achievement Tests
Level 5

Suitable for ages 11 – 13

Each test contains 35 mixed questions

- 15 general ability
- 10 reading comprehension
- 10 mathematics

A score summary chart is printed at the end of each test

Contents

Test 1	page 2
Test 2	page 13
Test 3	page 23
Test 4	page 34
Test 5	page 44

Solutions

Test 1	page 54
Test 2	page 55
Test 3	page 57
Test 4	page 59
Test 5	page 62

Copyright © 2017 Simon Steggels
All rights reserved

No part of this book may be reproduced, stored in a retrieval system, communicated or transmitted in any form or by any means without prior written permission. All inquiries should be made to the publisher.

ISBN 978-0-6480967-4-0

Published by
Advanced Instruction Pty Ltd
www.advancedinstruction.com.au

© MR STEGGELS ADVANCED INSTRUCTION PTY LTD

Test 1

Read the text and answer questions 1—5

Acropolis

An acropolis (from *ákros* meaning 'highest point' and *polis* meaning 'city') is the smaller core of a fortified city centre. It is built on elevated ground or a hill specifically chosen for defensive purposes.

The word acropolis is mainly associated with the Greek cities of Athens, Argos, Thebes and Corinth. But the term is applied more generally to all such fortified city centres found in many countries throughout the world, including Rome, Jerusalem, Asia Minor and Edinburgh. The term is also used to describe the overlapping plazas and pyramids in Maya cities. The ruins of Mission San Juan Capistrano's stone church in California are referred to as *The American Acropolis*. In Italy, small rural communities clustered at the base of a fortified area are known as *La Rocca*.

The most famous example is the Acropolis of Athens. In fact, it is universally known as *The Acropolis*. It is located on a flat-topped rock above the city of Athens and has a surface area of approximately three hectares. The remains of several ancient buildings are found here, including the Parthenon, a temple dedicated to the goddess Athena.

In the fifth century, Pericles, the prominent Greek statesmen and general of Athens, oversaw the construction of the Parthenon on the Acropolis. It was located in the centre. The Propylaea was a huge gateway at the entrance. The Temple of Athena Nike was located to the south of the entrance. The Erechtheum was a temple located to the north of the Parthenon. These buildings were severely damaged in 1687 during the Morean War when a cannonball hit stores of gunpowder in the Parthenon. To the south of the Acropolis was the Theatre of Dionysus.

A project to repair the Acropolis began in 1975. The aim was to reverse the damage caused by time, pollution, **attrition** and poor attempts at restoration. Original stone fragments were identified and reassembled. The colonnades that were destroyed by war were restored and placed in their proper location.

2 500 tonnes of original material, almost 700 reassembled stones and over 500 cubic metres of new marble were used in the restoration process. Valuable artifacts are housed in the Acropolis Museum that is located on the southern slope of the rock.

The Acropolis of Athens is a site of great architectural and historical significance.

© MR STEGGELS ADVANCED INSTRUCTION PTY LTD

1. The main purpose of the first paragraph is to

   A   provide important background information
   B   define the subject
   C   explain how something was made
   D   provide an orientation

2. Which word in the text means **strengthened against attack**?

   A   clustered
   B   defensive
   C   fortified
   D   restoration

3. Which word is most similar in meaning to **attrition**

   A   weathering
   B   weakening
   C   contrition
   D   erosion

4. Which building was not located on the flat top of The Acropolis?

   A   The Theatre of Dionysus
   B   The Temple of Athena Nike
   C   The Erechtheum
   D   The Propylaea

5. We can conclude that

   A   the term acropolis is used exclusively to refer to ruins in Greece
   B   Pericles continued to build the Acropolis after the Morean War
   C   restoration work focused on strengthening the Acropolis with new marble
   D   the Acropolis Museum was set up to house particularly important or fragile sculptures

© MR STEGGELS ADVANCED INSTRUCTION PTY LTD

6. Which word can be used to end the first word and begin the second?

    dist_____ / _____ear

    A   end
    B   ute
    C   ten
    D   pel

© MR STEGGELS ADVANCED INSTRUCTION PTY LTD

7. Which code should replace the question mark?

8. In a certain code **RAIN** and **RINK** are written **@47L** and **@7LY**. How would **AKIN** be written using the same code?

    A   4Y7@
    B   74YL
    C   4Y7L
    D   none of the above

9. Sam, Jen and I have saved a total of $1890. Sam saved one third as much money as Jen who saved six times more than I did. How much did money did Jen save?

    A $210
    B $630
    C $1260
    D $1420

© MR STEGGELS ADVANCED INSTRUCTION PTY LTD

This graph is for questions 10—11

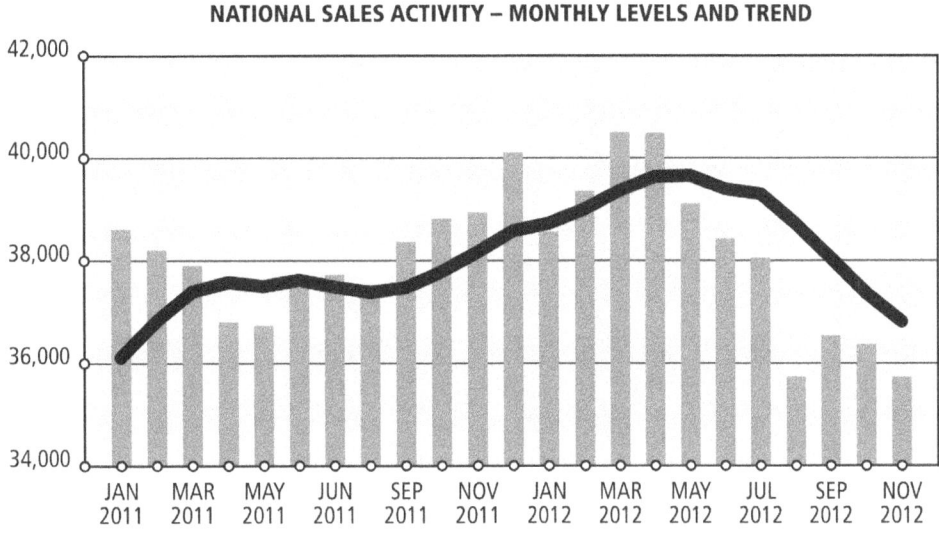

10. The graph indicates that average sales

    A   remained constant from March 2011 to November 2011
    B   began to fall in September 2011
    C   are returning to what they were two years earlier
    D   peaked in July 2012

11. The difference between the highest and lowest actual sales figures in this period is

    A   in between $6000 and $7000
    B   in between $5000 and $6000
    C   in between $4000 and $5000
    D   below $4000

12. **See** is to **seen** as **know** is to

    A   knew
    B   known
    C   knowing
    D   new

© MR STEGGELS ADVANCED INSTRUCTION PTY LTD

Read the text and answer questions 13—17

Key to the sounds of marked vowels

ā as in ate
ă as in bat
â as in care
à as in ask
ä as in arm
a̐ as in senate
e̐ as in event
ĕ as in maker
ē as in eve
ĕ as in met
ī as in kind
ĭ as in pin
ō as in note
ŏ as in not
ô as in or
o̐ as in obey
ū as in use
ŭ as in cut
û as in turn
u̐ as in unite
o͞o as in food
o͡o as in foot

© MR STEGGELS ADVANCED INSTRUCTION PTY LTD

13. The poet is mainly interested in

    A   spoken sound
    B   spelling
    C   phonetic symbols
    D   repetition

14. What technique does the poet use to create rhythm?

    A   repetition of the words **as in**
    B   alliteration—the first letter of a word is repeated
    C   onomatopoeia—a word sounds like the noise it is describing
    D   assonance—repetition of a vowel sound with different consonants

15. Which word also features the vowel sound u☐?

    A   untie
    B   put
    C   but
    D   cute

16. Which word also features the vowel sound å?

    A   cast
    B   swarm
    C   pack
    D   cave

17. We can conclude that this poem is

    A   meant to be funny
    B   intended to be spoken aloud
    C   is intended to assist students with speech difficulties
    D   not meant to make sense

18. Which is the odd one out?

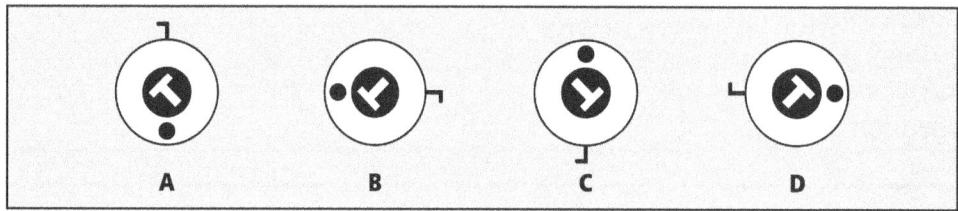

19. What is meant by the phrase **through thick and thin**?

    A   through both thick and thin consistencies
    B   to support someone regardless of their level of intelligence
    C   to support someone regardless of physical appearance
    D   despite all obstacles and adversity

20. Which figure should replace the question mark in the following sequence?

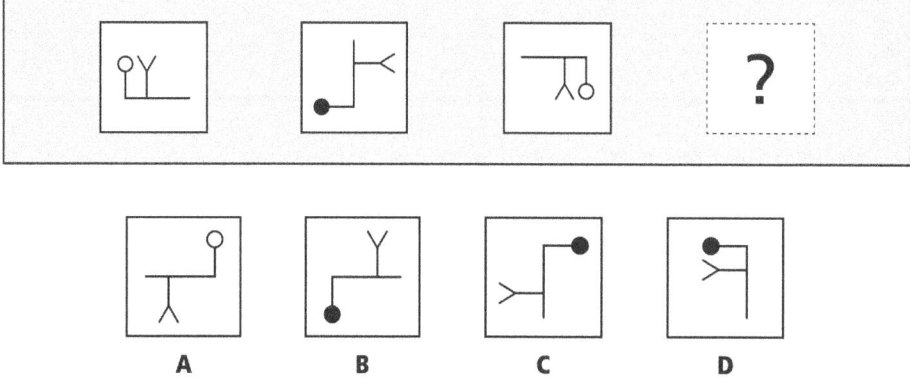

© MR STEGGELS ADVANCED INSTRUCTION PTY LTD

21. A farmer uses one quarter of his farm for peaches, two fifths for nectarines and one tenth for lemons. He uses the remaining 10 hectares for tomatoes. What is the total area of his farm?

    A   20 hectares
    B   30 hectares
    C   40 hectares
    D   60 hectares

22. Which word is not like the other three?

    A   silk
    B   nylon
    C   wool
    D   cotton

23. Which is the odd one out?

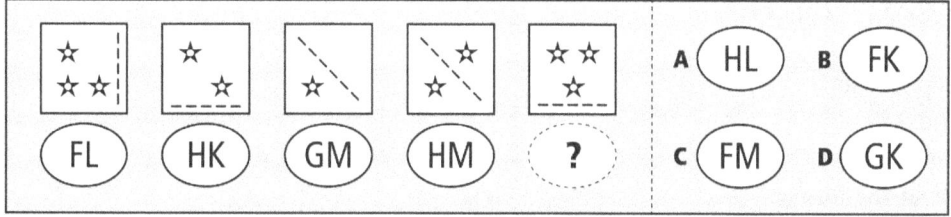

24. There were 200 pieces of fruit in a sorting bin. 30% were peaches. When some peaches were picked from the bin, the percentage of peaches fell to 20%. How many peaches were picked from the bin?

    A   60
    B   40
    C   20
    D   25

© MR STEGGELS ADVANCED INSTRUCTION PTY LTD

25. The word most opposite to **mild** is

    A   bland
    B   mellow
    C   sweet
    D   sharp

26. Which letter is the odd one out?

| P | A | X | M | U |

    A   P
    B   A
    C   M
    D   U

27. Another word for **theory** is

    A   hypothesis
    B   guess
    C   assumption
    D   all of the above

28. The average temperature for the period shown is closest to

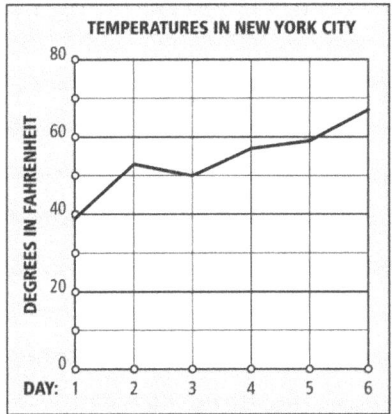

    A   45°F
    B   50°F
    C   54°F
    D   56°F

29. Which number should replace the question mark?

4	6	2	8	7	3
7	10	1	12	9	?

- A   0
- B   1
- C   6
- D   There is no pattern

30. A car rental company charges $57.80 per day to hire a car, plus 15cents for each kilometre. I rented a car for eight days and drove 860km. What was the total cost for car hire?

- A $475.30
- B $518.70
- C $591.40
- D $708.60

31. Complete the following sentence by choosing the correct words

         A _____ contains _____ with similar _____ .

- A   thesaurus / synonyms / antonyms
- B   dictionary / words / definitions
- C   textbook / topics / answers
- D   thesaurus / lists of words / meanings

32. A 10L bucket is half full of water. The water evaporates after 20 days. Another bucket has 7L of water. How many days will it take to evaporate if the water in both buckets evaporates at the same rate?

- A   14 days
- B   28 days
- C   49 days
- D   60 days

© MR STEGGELS ADVANCED INSTRUCTION PTY LTD

33. I entered the freeway at 7:30am and exited at 8:15am. In that time I covered 63km. What was my average speed?

    A   84mk/h
    B   98km/h
    C   108km/h
    D   impossible to calculate given only this information

34. **Neck** is to **scarf** as **head** is to

    A   toga
    B   fez
    C   camisole
    D   espadrille

35. Which tile should replace the question mark in this sequence?

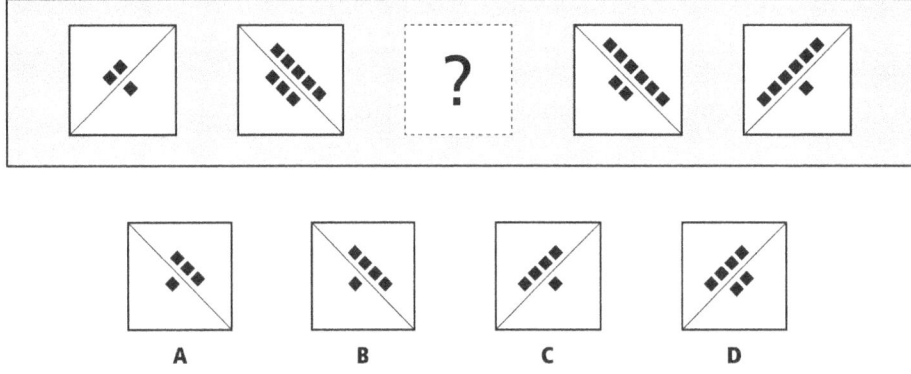

© MR STEGGELS ADVANCED INSTRUCTION PTY LTD

END OF TEST

Test 2

1. The prime numbers between 20 and 50 total

    A   204
    B   250
    C   251
    D   none of the above

2. Which word is closest in meaning to **pacify**?

    A   appease
    B   serve
    C   pacific
    D   peaceful

3. I bought a coat and a pair of shoes. The shoes were 40% of the cost of the coat. The coat was $312 more than the shoes. How much did I spend altogether?

    A $352
    B $361
    C $520
    D $728

4. Tammy and I had a total of 48 marbles. After I bought another 6, Tammy had five times as many as me. How many marbles did I have to begin with?

    A   3
    B   6
    C   9
    D   45

© MR STEGGELS ADVANCED INSTRUCTION PTY LTD

Read the text and answer questions 5—9

Glossary of terms	
AAC	Advanced Audio Coding is an audio compression algorithm that uses a form of data compression. Designed to replace MP3, AAC generally achieves better sound quality at similar bitrates. While the .aac extension is sometimes used for AAC-encoded files, they are saved with an .m4a file extension.
bitrate	The quality of an audio or video file. For audio data the bitrate is commonly measured in Kbps. An MP3 audio file that is compressed at 192 Kbps will have a greater dynamic range and sound clearer than the same audio file compressed at 128 Kbps.
bpm	Beats per minute is used as a measure of tempo in music. Higher bpm = faster tempo
codec	Short for compressor/decompressor, a codec is any technology for compressing and decompressing audio and video data. An example is MP3.
crossfader	The crossfader is a slider that determines how much each deck of audio contributes to the master output.
cueing	Headphone cueing is listening in your headphones to the next track you would like to mix in. The audience cannot hear what you are cueing in your headphones. This is a crucial aspect to DJing.
db	Short for decibels. A decibel is a logarithmic measurement of sound level. Whispering is around 25 dB while unbearable sound such as a jet engine is around 160 db. A volume increase of 10 dB is perceived as twice as loud.
deck	a virtual turntable that a track can be loaded into and played.
head/mix button	Used to control how much of the master output is mixed into your headphones. You are able to test out how it sounds when mixed with the main mix in your headphones, before letting the audience hear the track.
level meter	Used to show volume levels of audio signals. The level should average around the top of the green region, with the loudest parts of the music in the yellow region. If the level meter is in the red region, the volume should be turned down.
MIDI	Musical Instrument Digital Interface—a digital language and hardware specification that allows compatible electronic instruments, sequencers, computers to communicate with each other in a network.
phase	The position of a track (song) compared to another track. If two tracks are in sync, they are being played at the same tempo and phase. The beats of both tracks are aligned.
sync	Allows you to automatically adjust tempo and phase to sync two tracks
vinyl control	A method that simulates the traditional DJing on two turntables. Using special time code media, the DJ application analyses the time code signal and simulates the sound and feel of vinyl.

5. This text would most probably be included in

    A   a policy statement
    B   a scientific report
    C   an instruction manual
    D   an editorial

6. If two tracks are in synch then

    A   the beats of both tracks are aligned
    B   they are being played at the same tempo
    C   they are in the same phase
    D   all of the above

7. What enables communication between compatible hardware?

    A   cueing
    B   AAC
    C   sync control
    D   MIDI

8. We can conclude that this information applies to DJs who use

    A   only traditional turntables and vinyl records
    B   mainly digital mixing software
    C   both turntables and vinyl records at the same time as digital mixing software
    D   virtual turntables, vinyl records and MIDI software

9. Which is true?

    A   codec is an audio compression algorithm that uses only a form of data compression
    B   DJs use headphone cueing to synch a new track that cannot be heard by the audience
    C   The .m4a file extension is deigned to replace AAC encoded files
    D   The average volume level should be in the yellow region

© MR STEGGELS ADVANCED INSTRUCTION PTY LTD

10. A train travelled ⅓ of its journey at 60km/h and completed the remaining 180km in three hours. What was the total time taken for the journey?

    A   3⅓ hours
    B   4.5 hours
    C   5 hours
    D   6.5 hours

11. Which code should replace the question mark?

12. Which word can be placed before these words to make new, compound words?

    _____hill   _____hold   _____note   _____bridge

    A   over
    B   foot
    C   high
    D   small

13. The letters in **freed** can be rearranged to make a new word meaning

    A   surrender
    B   released
    C   watched
    D   postpone

14. All Zeds are red. Some Woxs are yellow and some are red. No Yips are red, brown or yellow. Xuds are never red or yellow; some are brown and some are blue. Therefore

    A   some Zeds are Xuds
    B   some Yips are Woxs
    C   some Zeds are Yips
    D   some Yips are Xuds

15. **Cue** is to **queue** as **marshal** is to

    A   marital
    B   martial
    C   sheriff
    D   marque

16. This graph describes the movement of a bicycle

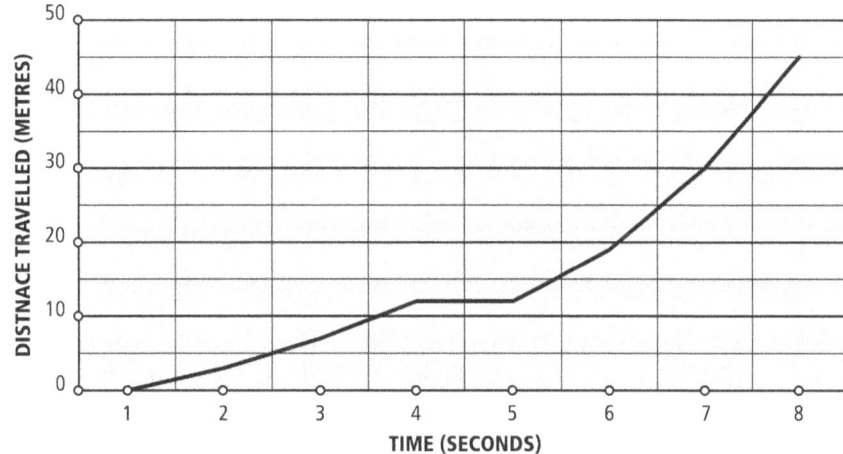

Which statement is true?

    A   The bicycle slows down briefly before picking up speed after 5 seconds
    B   The bicycle travels at a constant speed
    C   The bicycle is travelling at 5m per second
    D   none of the above

© MR STEGGELS ADVANCED INSTRUCTION PTY LTD

17. I have a pile of pencils. If I group them in bundles of 8, I have five left over. If I group them in bundles of 9, one group will be four pencils short. How many pencils do I have?

    A   72
    B   74
    C   76
    D   77

18. In a certain code, **made**, **name** and **dean** are written **bxpt**, **qpbx** and **tpqx** but not necessarily in that order. How would **mend** be written using this code?

    A   bxqp
    B   qxbp
    C   qxtb
    D   qxbt

19. Which code should replace the question mark?

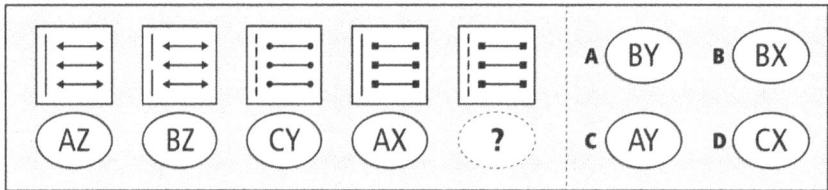

20. I had 196 marbles. I gave $^2/_7$ of them to my friend Sam. Then I gave $^2/_7$ of what was left to my friend Carol. I then gave $^2/_5$ of what was left to my friend Julie. How many marbles did I keep?

    A   60
    B   40
    C   80
    D   50

21. Which number should replace the question mark?

| 2 | 3 | 5 | 7 | 11 | ? |

    A   13
    B   14
    C   16
    D   there is no pattern

22. Which is the odd one out?

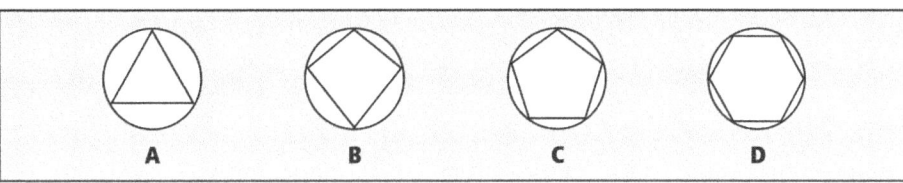

23. Choose the pair of words that best completes the following sentence

Australia has many ☐ spots. Bondi Beach is a favourite ☐ for many travellers.

A	scenic	spot
B	holiday	place
C	popular	time
D	tourist	destination

24. **Jean** is to **Jane** as **Ronald** is to

A Donald
B Arnold
C Renald
D McDonald

25. I bought a shirt for $36. It had been reduced by 25%. What was the original selling price?

A $54
B $52
C $48
D $45

26. In a certain code, the words **post**, **soap**, **tape** and **step** are written **3281**, **4817**, **3471** and **1234**, but not necessarily in that order. How would the words **pesto paste** be written?

A 17432 18437
B 17348 18347
C 17342 18342
D none of the above

Read the text and answer questions 27—31

Necromancy

The widow's son in zealous zeal with windward witchery
Winds the mellow horn
As the world throngs beneath with unwilling feet

The wild little poet his weary heart unfolds
In visionary hours
Voracious and vulnerable in vermillion vestments
Unwonted, untainted, unfought victories won
Unconquerable, unfeigned, unfettered

Delivers his **supplicating** sermon
To silent ghosts in misty shrouds shambling to the sepulcher
Its rightful inhabitants, the riggers of death

Prodigious apparitions
Harpies of the shore
A prophecy, a preface, the pain of a fearful curse

The meteor of the ocean air in meshes of steel
Measured in cups of ale
The intoxication of invention
In points of likeness unexact

Their fugitive sovereign from hiding emerges

27. The main goal of the widow's son is to

    A   wind the mellow horn
    B   deliver a supplicating sermon to silent ghosts
    C   to summon the fugitive sovereign from hiding
    D   unleash his blackened heart

28. The poet has used alliteration in the second stanza

    A   to increase the rhythm of the poem
    B   because these are the words used in a conjuring spell
    C   to build drama
    D   for comic effect

29. Which words from the poem are most similar in meaning?

    A   unwonted   untainted
    B   voracious   vulnerable
    C   spirits   apparitions
    D   prophecy   curse

30. Choose the best meaning for **supplicating**

    A   ask or beg for something humbly
    B   attempting to make someone less angry or hostile
    C   to express disapproval of
    D   exciting or stirring

31. We can conclude that **necromancy** is

    A   a form of magic involving communication with and summoning of spirits
    B   witchcraft aimed at using the deceased as a weapon
    C   a form of black magic—the use of supernatural powers for evil purposes
    D   all of the above

© MR STEGGELS ADVANCED INSTRUCTION PTY LTD

32. Unscramble the following groups of letters and choose the word that means **a type of musical instrument** and **a mathematical figure**

    A   deercorr
    B   mertutp
    C   rateling
    D   gateponn

33. The phrase **dark horse** refers to a person who

    A   is new to the group or area
    B   shows potential in the beginning but who fails to deliver in the end
    C   takes a position in an argument without believing in that position
    D   was previously unknown but who has now come to prominence

34. I am thinking of a word that means

    (1) a type of fish
    (2) a resting place in a high position

    This word begins with the letter

    A   s
    B   p
    C   f
    D   t

35. I made a rectangle from a 26cm piece of wire. One side is 2cm longer than the other. What is the area of the rectangle?

    A $143cm^2$
    B $52cm^2$
    C $41.25cm^2$
    D $412.50cm^2$

© MR STEGGELS ADVANCED INSTRUCTION PTY LTD

END OF TEST

Test 3

1. One apple and one banana costs $4. I bought 8 apples and 6 bananas and spent $29. My friend bought 6 apples and 8 bananas. How much did he spend?

   A $25
   B $27
   C $31
   D $48

2. The word **avid** is closest in meaning to

   A   aware
   B   eager
   C   apathetic
   D   shrewd

3. What is the missing section in this puzzle?

4	3	5	4	6
2		3	2	4
3	2		3	5
1		2	1	3
2		3	2	4

   A: 1, 4, 0, 1
   B: 1, 5, 1, 0
   C: 0, 4, 0, 1
   D: 0, 5, 1, 0

4. Four boys competed to see who was the fastest sprinter over 100m. They raced twice.

   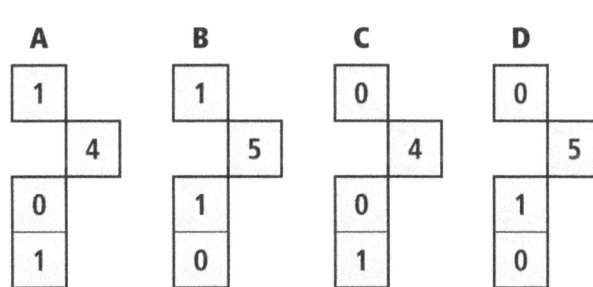

   Andy was never last. | Col always beat Dean. | Benjamin had at least **1** 1st place. | Andy finished **3rd** in at least **1** of the races. | Both Dean and Col had a **2nd** place.

   How did they finish?

   A   Race 1: Andy, Benjamin, Col, Dean   Race 2: Benjamin, Col, Andy, Dean
   B   Race 1: Benjamin, Col, Andy, Dean   Race 2: Col, Dean, Andy, Benjamin
   C   Race 1: Benjamin, Col, Andy, Dean   Race 2: Benjamin, Dean, Andy, Col
   D   Race 1: Andy, Dean, Col, Benjamin   Race 2: Benjamin, Col, Dean, Andy

© MR STEGGELS ADVANCED INSTRUCTION PTY LTD

5. Which numbers are missing from the pattern?

    | 1 | 1 | 3 | 3 | 6 | 7 | 10 | 13 | 15 | 21 | | |

    A   21, 31
    B   21, 28
    C   27, 30
    D   There is no pattern

6. Which is the odd one out?

    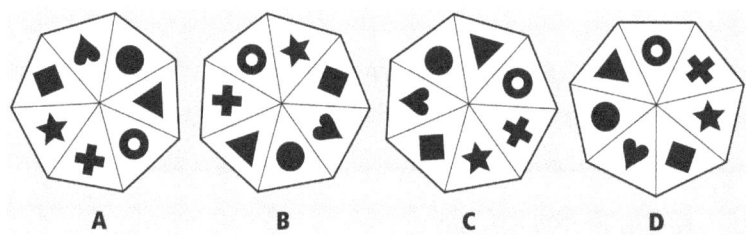

7. Which pair of words is most opposite in meaning?

    A   superlative   ordinary
    B   crucial   traumatic
    C   subversive   uncommitted
    D   innovative   scarce

8. Seven friends went out for dinner. The bill came to $330.30. Abbey and Brian each paid ⅙ of the bill. Cathy paid ⅕ more than Abbey. Dennis paid 10% of the total. Enid put in $30 and wanted $4 change. Frank paid 1.5 times what Enid paid. Gina paid the remainder of the bill which was

    A $62.16
    B $59.11
    C $56.11
    D   none of the above

© MR STEGGELS ADVANCED INSTRUCTION PTY LTD

9. Which pair of words is closest in meaning?

    A   level   fundamental
    B   meteoric   spectacular
    C   exemplary   consummate
    D   flawed   impeccable

10. Which net matches the cube?

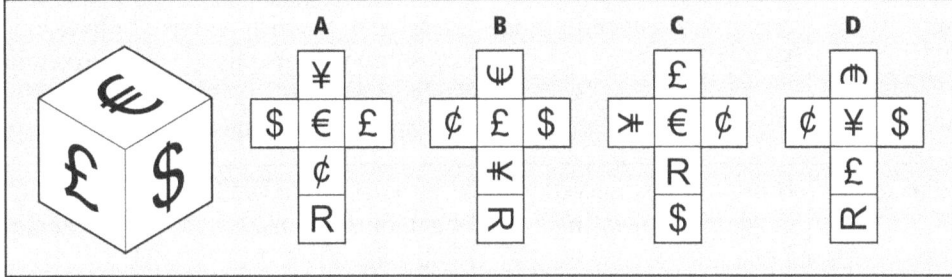

11. In a certain code, **lazy** is written **ynml**. How would **white** be written using the same code?

    A   juvrg
    B   juvgs
    C   jvugr
    D   juvgr

12. There were 289 people at a school concert. ⅝ of the females in the audience were girls. Boys made up ⅔ of male audience members. There were an equal number of women and men at the concert. How many men were at the concert?

    A   17
    B   32
    C   51
    D   97

© MR STEGGELS ADVANCED INSTRUCTION PTY LTD

Read the text and answer questions 13 -17

Wood Fire Pizzeria Menu		19 Fintus St Hokgate		**Call 9310 7711**
STARTERS		TRADITIONAL PIZZA		S $12 R $14 L $17
Zaatar: dried thyme, sesame seeds, olive oil, topped with a bruschchetta salsa S $6 R $8	Feta: Bulgarian feta, olives, oregano S $7 R $9	Margarita: tomatoes, basil & mozzarella		Pepperoni: sliced spicy pepperoni & mozzarella
Garlic: garlic base with mozzarella cheese S $6 R $8	Wedges: served with sour cream & sweet chilli sauce $9	Supreme: leg ham, capsicum, Spanish onions, mushrooms, cabanossi, kalamata olives, mozzarella and achovies		Napolitana: kalamata olives, anchovies & mozzarella
Salt & pepper squid: served with homemade mayonnaise $12	Buffalo wings: served with tangy, ranch dressing $12	Capriciossa: shaved leg ham, mushrooms, kalamata olives & mozzarella		Hawaiian: leg ham, pineapple & mozzarella
MEAT S $16 R $18 L $21		CHICKEN S $16 R $18 L $21		
BBQ meat lovers: marinated ground beef, leg ham, BBQ sauce, pepperoni, cabanossi, bacon & mozzarella	Lamb: marinated lamb, balsamic vinegar, onions, feta, rocket, zesty dressing	Chilli: grilled free range chicken, kalamata olives, shallots, sundried tomatoes, pine nuts, chilli oil & mozzarella		Pesto: pesto base, grilled free range chicken, kalamata olives, sundried tomatoes & mozzarella
Chorizo: sliced chorizo, Bulgarian feta, baby spinach & sundried tomatoes	Antipasto: oven roasted eggplant, prosciutto, leg ham, Danish salami, chorizo, caramelised onion, sundried tomatoes, olives, gorgonzola & mozzarella	BBQ chicken: BBQ sauce base, grilled free range chicken, mushrooms, grilled capsicum, Spanish onion, pineapple & mozzarella		Peri Peri: grilled free range chicken, tomatoes, shallots, capsicum, Spanish onion, mozzarella & peri peri sauce
VEGETARIAN S $15 R $17 L $20		SEAFOOD S $17 R $19 L $22		
Fresh: baby spinach, cherry tomatoes, kalamata olives, parmesan, balsamic vinegarette, oregano & mozzarella	Formaggio: mozzarella, bannoncini, Bulgarian feta & parmesan cheese	The sea: garlic marinated king prawns, pepper scallops, shallots, capsicum, tomatoes, lemon		Garlic prawn: marinated garlic king prawns & mozzarella topped with avocado
PASTA $14		SALADS $10		
Chicken pesto penne Fettuccine bosciola Spaghetti bolognaise	Penne arrabiatta Fettuccine chilli Prawn	Greek Chicken Caesar Rocket & parmesan		Garden Basil and buffalo Mozzarella
We deliver with Pizza Express!	**Opening Hours: Tues-Sun 3pm—10pm**	**½ & ½ pizza available on Large $2 extra**		**Gluten free base $3**

© MR STEGGELS ADVANCED INSTRUCTION PTY LTD

13. Which item on the menu has Bulgarian feta?

    A   Feta
    B   Chorizo
    C   Formaggio
    D   all of the above

14. How many items on the menu have kalamata olives?

    A   three
    B   four
    C   six
    D   seven

15. Which pizza has the fewest ingredients?

    A   Hawaiian
    B   Napolitana
    C   Pepperoni
    D   Margarita

16. I ordered a large gluten free ½ Garlic Prawn ½ The Sea pizza, penne arrabiatta, wedges and a Greek salad. What change should I receive from $100?

    A $40
    B $45
    C $53
    D $60

17. What is the most common ingredient used at Wood Fire Pizzeria?

    A   kalamata olives
    B   garlic
    C   mozzarella
    D   leg ham

© MR STEGGELS ADVANCED INSTRUCTION PTY LTD

18. Which tile completes the pattern?

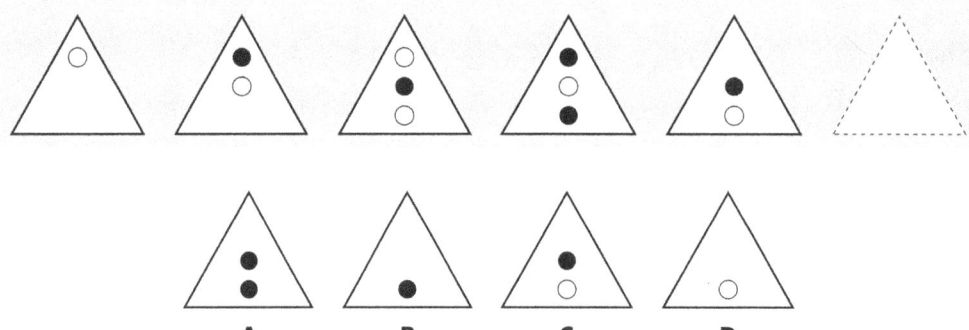

19. **Frail** is to **robustness** as

   A   long-winded is to brevity
   B   humorous is to geniality
   C   mild is to mellowness
   D   blunt is to obtuseness

20. My petrol tank gauge is 0.375. How much petrol has been used if the tank capacity is 1224L?

   A   153L
   B   408L
   C   459L
   D   765L

21. In a certain code, **xzsbdefgaectay** is **seat**. In the same code, **hgalnltqpomski** is

   A   hams
   B   gems
   C   alps
   D   ants

© MR STEGGELS ADVANCED INSTRUCTION PTY LTD

22. A train travelled for the first four hours of its journey at an average speed of 88km/h. Its average speed for the remaining five hours of the journey was 52km/h. What was the average speed of the train for the entire journey?

    A   70km/h
    B   68km/h
    C   88km/h
    D   impossible to calculate given only this information

23. Which proverbs are closest in meaning?

    (1) a miss is as good as a mile
    (2) a nod is as good as a wink
    (3) a rose is a rose is a rose
    (4) to call a spade a spade

    A   3 and 4
    B   1 and 3
    C   2 and 3
    D   1 and 4

24. I had 700 marbles. They were red and blue. I sold ⅓ of the red marbles and bought 20 more blue marbles. Then I had 6 times more red than blue marbles. How many more red than blue marbles were there at first?

    A   648
    B   596
    C   500
    D   72

25. Rearrange the group of words to make a coherent sentence, with the subject at the beginning

    through   the   in   child   below   onto   the   gap   the   floor   the   sand   fell

    The last word in the sentence is

    A   sand
    B   below
    C   gap
    D   child

© MR STEGGELS ADVANCED INSTRUCTION PTY LTD

Read the text and answer questions 26—30

All my troubles began when my pest of a brother, Charlie, got a forensic science kit for his tenth birthday from Uncle Troy, and he and his best friend, Melvin Dooley, started thinking they were detectives. The kit looked just like a regular toolbox. It came with everything they needed to start a crime laboratory of their own. As well as an inkpad for taking fingerprints and a bottle of black dusting powder and brush, there was a flashlight, plastic gloves, tweezers, scissors, two magnifying glasses, a casting kit for tyres and shoe impressions, rolls of transparent tape and plastic bags with the word *Evidence* printed on them in black. There was even a set of plastic handcuffs. For a kids' toy, it looked pretty professional. Maybe a little too professional…

Charlie wanted to fingerprint everyone in the house right away, including Nan's cat, Tibby. But when he tried to press her paw onto the inkpad, she scratched him and took off outside. Serves him right. Whoever heard of a cat with a police record?

Nan volunteered to have her prints taken first. Charlie inked her fingers then rolled each one carefully from side to side onto a fingerprint card. 'You look just like a real policeman doing that,' she told him. 'I feel like a criminal already.'

Dad muttered something under his breath but he wouldn't repeat it. 'Just clearing my throat,' he said. Nan narrowed her eyes at him.

'See the wave-like patterns?' Charlie asked Nan, handing her a magnifying glass. 'They're called arches, and the lines that go back on themselves—they're loops.'

'What about those?' Nan asked, pointing at her fingerprint card. 'The lines that look like swirls.'

'They're called whorls,' Charlie replied. 'Dad has some of those too but his aren't the same as yours. No two sets of fingerprints are ever the same. It says here in my handbook that identical twins have exactly the same DNA but different fingerprints because their phenotype is different from their genotype. That's interesting, isn't it?'

'Fascinating,' Nan said.

I yawned loudly.

Charlie peered at me over the top of his handbook. 'You'd better pay attention, Laura,' he said. 'Some day you'll be getting fingerprinted all over again, but it won't be pretend—you'll be a real criminal.'

I scowled at him. 'This ink had better come off my fingers before we go back to school. I don't want everyone thinking I'm some sort of juvenile delinquent.'

Tibby gave Charlie a wide berth after he'd tried to fingerprint her paws. She hid beneath the lounge, eyeing him with suspicion each time he came into the living room. Clearly, his new detective hobby was making her nervous. And she wasn't the only one.

Later in the kitchen, Dad took Nan aside. 'I don't know why Troy bought Charlie that kit,' he said. 'Being a policeman and dealing with the criminal underclass everyday, I thought he would've had more sense.'

'Oh Gregory, will you relax?' Nan said. 'The boys are just having a little fun, plus they're learning new things.'

'Yes—learning new ways to get into trouble,' Dad said. 'Mark my words, kids and crime don't mix.'

26. Choose the best definition of the word **forensic** as it is used in the text

    A   an action or omission which constitutes an offence and is punishable by law
    B   relating to courts of law and criminal procedures
    C   the application of scientific methods to the investigation of crime
    D   concerning crime and its investigation

27. The name of the narrator is

    A   Charlie
    B   Dad
    C   Laura
    D   it doesn't say in the text

28. We can conclude that Nan narrowed her eyes at Dad because he

    A   was just clearing his throat
    B   wouldn't repeat what he said under his breath
    C   disapproved of Charlie's new hobby
    D   muttered a sarcastic comment about Nan being a criminal

29. Choose the most suitable question for the following answer

    No two sets of fingerprints are ever the same

    A   Why is fingerprinting so important in identifying an individual criminal?
    B   Why are arches, loops and whorls looked at closely when identifying fingerprints?
    C   What is the difference between someone's phenotype and their genotype?
    D   Why do identical twins have different fingerprints?

30. What is the purpose of the ellipsis (…) in the following sentence

    Maybe a little too professional…

    A   It demonstrates a pause in the narrative
    B   It makes up for a missing piece of text
    C   The narrator is leaving a thought unfinished
    D   It suggests that the kit is an inappropriate toy

© MR STEGGELS ADVANCED INSTRUCTION PTY LTD

31. A train travelled at 96km/h. If it left Central Terminal at 9:45am, at what time did it reach its destination 336km away?

    A   12:15pm
    B   12:45pm
    C   1:15pm
    D   1:45pm

32. Which word does not rhyme with the other three?

    A   mauve
    B   grove
    C   hove
    D   shove

33. The letters **lctooe** can be rearranged to make the name of **a member of the feline family**.

    The name begins with the letter

    A   l
    B   c
    C   e
    D   o

34. Which of these statements is incorrect?

    A   2349 = 9
    B   1065 = 3
    C   2645 = 8
    D   8173 = 7

© MR STEGGELS ADVANCED INSTRUCTION PTY LTD

35. This chart shows minimum and maximum temperatures for six different locations on a single day

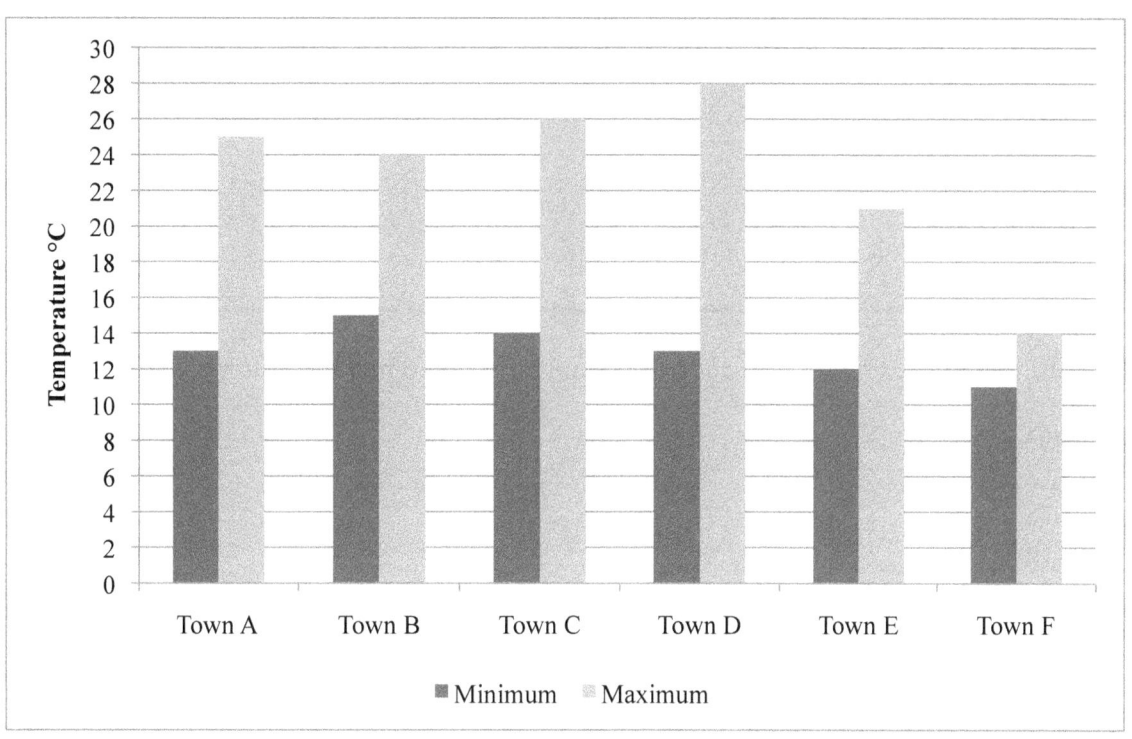

The difference between the average maximum and the average minimum for all locations is

A   10°C
B   13°C
C   23°C
D   60°C

END OF TEST

Test 4

1. A ladder 10m in length rests against a wall. If the foot of the ladder is 6m away from the wall, how far up the wall does the ladder reach?

    A   4m
    B   6m
    C   8m
    D   impossible to calculate given only this information

2. A 6cm cube had a hole of side 3cm cut right through it. The remaining volume was

    A $189cm^3$
    B $162cm^3$
    C $207cm^3$
    D $27cm^3$

3. Rearrange the letters in **raccoon** to make a word meaning **circles of light around a luminous body**

    The new word begins with

    A   c
    B   r
    C   a
    D   o

4. Unscramble the following words and choose which one is **not a bird**

    A   brino
    B   wifts
    C   aglee
    D   rashk

© MR STEGGELS ADVANCED INSTRUCTION PTY LTD

5. If you unscramble **ohnacpi** and add a letter, you can make a new word that means **victor**.

   The letter than must be added is

   A   d
   B   g
   C   y
   D   m

6. Which tile completes the pattern?

   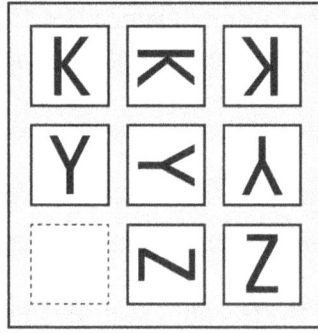

7. The first, last and two middle pages of a book add to 986. How many pages are there in the book?

   A   between 500 and 495
   B   between 495 and 490
   C   between 490 and 485
   D   less than 485

8. Rearrange the letters in the phrase **risen to recur** to make a word meaning **restored to life**.

   This new word begins with the letter

   A   s
   B   r
   C   t
   D   e

Read the text and answer questions 9—13

The Candela V Beam Perfecta Laser selectively targets the skin using an intense burst of yellow light. Blood vessels in the skin absorb the light. This helps to stimulate new collagen formation. Skin can be 'remodelled' in this way.

The Candela V Beam Perfecta Laser treats redness of the face and neck, broken capillaries, spider naevi, rosacea, port wine stains and some birthmarks, sun/age spots, early scars and stretchmarks, fine lines and wrinkles; as well as mild acne scarring.

The Candela Vbeam Perfecta laser uses a special Dynamic Cooling Device (DCD) to deliver a very cold spray to the skin just before the laser pulse is emitted. This helps to reduce discomfort during treatment, and also protect the top layers of the skin. Each pulse feels like an elastic band being 'snapped' against the skin. There may be some warmth. An anaesthetic cream, if required, will be applied to the area at least one hour before the procedure.

Pulsed dye lasers have been successfully used for over thirty years to treat birthmarks. Laser technology has improved greatly so side effects are minimal. There will be some discomfort during the procedure. Immediately after treatment, skin will appear red, and swollen, similar to mild sunburn. There may also be some bruising, depending on the condition being treated and the treatment settings. An ice pack is used in the 24 hours following treatment to help reduce swelling, which will disappear over a period of 3 to 5 days. Bruising will disappear in 7-14 days. Make-up can be applied to the treated areas providing that it is applied and removed very gently. There may also be some lightening or darkening of the skin in the treated areas, thinning of the skin and scarring.

Sun exposure must be avoided before and for 6 weeks after treatment to minimise side effects. An SPF 30+ sunscreen must be worn daily. This helps to reduce the risk of temporary brown pigmentation (increase in skin colour), which will take months to fade. Gently cleanse the treatment area and apply a thin smear of moisturiser daily until healed. Avoid facial scrubs and irritating creams, especially retinols and sulphur based products. Is it best to avoid intense exercise for 1-2 weeks following treatment.

Patients typically notice improvement in their skin within 6-8 weeks. The skin may also be firmer and tighter due to the stimulation of new collagen production. Patients with facial redness and blood vessels will usually require 2-3 treatments. Patients with port-wine stains may need 6-10 treatments. Patients with acne scarring and fine lines and wrinkles may need up to 6 treatments.

Patients are provided with an estimate of the treatment cost at the time of consultation. There may be a tax rebate for the treatment of port wine stains and birthmarks, and for some patients with redness or broken capillaries on the head and neck. Private health funds typically do not cover treatment.

© MR STEGGELS ADVANCED INSTRUCTION PTY LTD

9. Which is true?

    A   The Perfecta Laser uses a special cooling device just after the laser pulse is emitted
    B   Make-up cannot be applied to the treated areas for 3 to 5 days following treatment
    C   Port wine stains require more treatments than facial redness and broken capillaries
    D   All Perfecta Laser treatments attract a tax rebate

10. Paragraph four is mainly about

    A   precautions to be taken
    B   the treatment procedure
    C   the history of laser technology
    D   side effects of treatment

11. Skin will feel tighter following treatment with Perfecta Laser because

    A   the skin will appear red and swollen, similar to a mild sunburn
    B   an ice pack is used in the 24 hours following treatment to reduce swelling
    C   new collagen production is stimulated
    D   each pulse feels like an elastic band being snapped against the skin

12. Which words from the text are used interchangeably?

    A   red   swollen
    B   treatment   procedure
    C   firmer   tighter
    D   applied   reduce

13. We can conclude that it is best to avoid intense exercise following treatment because

    A   sun exposure must be avoided for six weeks to minimise side effects
    B   the skin will be bruised for up to two weeks
    C   exercise increases blood flow to the skin, which will increase redness
    D   all of the above

© MR STEGGELS ADVANCED INSTRUCTION PTY LTD

14. Signposts appear on a bike track in a special pattern—every 1km, 2km, 4km, 7km and so on. The closest sign to the 200km mark is at

    A   191km
    B   192km
    C   210km
    D   211km

15. In a certain code, the word **mixed** is written **kkvgb**. In the same code, **plant** is written

    A   rjclv
    B   nnypr
    C   nmxrp
    D   rncpv

16. Which pair of words is closest in meaning?

    A   infamy   disrepute
    B   tepid   timid
    C   secret   secrete
    D   discharge   absorb

17. A tank in the shape of a cube, with sides measuring 10m, is half-filled with water. A concrete block of volume 125m^3 is then placed in the tank. What will be the height of the water in the tank?

    A   1.25m
    B   3.75m
    C   5.0m
    D   6.25m

18. **Southern** is to **ocean** as **Coral** is to

    A   reef
    B   sea
    C   organism
    D   bleaching

19. What is the chance of rolling triple 5 with three, six-sided dice?

    A   1 out of 15
    B   1 out of 125
    C   1 out of 216
    D   1 out of 555

20. Which word is most similar in meaning to **sulk**?

    A   soak
    B   bawl
    C   brood
    D   fret

21. Which number completes the pattern?

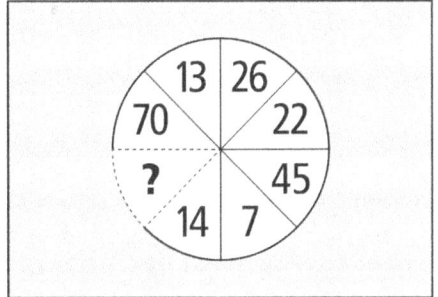

    A   3
    B   11
    C   35
    D   there is no pattern

22. Which is the best buy for pet food?

    A   0.75kg for $1.35
    B   0.5kg for $0.90
    C   1.5kg for $2.60
    D   2.0kg for $3.50

© MR STEGGELS ADVANCED INSTRUCTION PTY LTD

Read the text and answer questions 23—27

My visit to the canyon

I was at first perhaps overly enthusiastic about my trip to the canyon. I had wandered to other scenes, because the anticipation of witnessing for the first time something truly extraordinary, that comprised all the wonder of nature, left me loathe to exchange my personal treasure trove of hope for that of a faint memory.

I trembled with dread as the moment drew nearer. But the instant was still in futurity. I stepped down from the carriage with perfect composure, handed my coat to the porter, indicated my suitcase, and inquired not the quickest route to the viewing platform, but the readiness of my accommodations; not the most advantageous position to view the enormity of the canyon but the likely change in the weather given that the dinner hour was close at hand. Too often, when the object of one's desire is placed within reach, a sense of disappointment, even apathy arises. And excuses are found in order to delay the moment of inevitability; the risk of even further disappointment.

I chose the left-hand path that wended away from the hotel entrance and followed it to the edge of the great American ravine. It was an afternoon of immense sunshine; cloudless, save some wisps of white at dizzying heights. I closed my eyes and imagined falling headlong into the canyon from height to depth. I stationed myself in the blast of hot air that rose from below. The earth was tremulous beneath me. I looked along the abyss and tried to understand it in one immeasurable idea. After half an hour spent motionless, I left the rocky outcrop, and by a staircase, descended to the viewing platform below. The path lay over fragments of cliffs.

Summoned to an unknown wonder, approaching the brink, warned of my own mortality, haunted by a vision of endless depth, tumbling down out of the sky. I struggled to adapt to this new reality. The vastness of the canyon crippled all human accomplishment. The huge expanse of time spent gouging in solid earth a canyon so immense, crushed all ambition. I was filled with equal parts awe and dread. The mighty scene captured the destiny of all living things. I was merely a transient, no more than vapour rising into thin air above everlasting rock.

My thoughts were interrupted by a group of observers keen to take in their first view of the canyon. The first to thrust a head forward over the precipice was a tall, pale man who looked somewhat akin to an undertaker. Seemingly unaffected by the magnificent panorama, he raised his eyebrows faintly and turned away to blow his nose. His wife, a short, ruddy woman, declared that, upon the whole, the canyon was rather deep and worth looking at. She wondered aloud if the chef would be serving fish. Then she gave herself over to the enjoyment of a bar of chocolate that she had pulled from her handbag.

The time finally came to return to the hotel. The sun was near setting and the air turned cool. The base of the canyon was swimming in deep purple shadow. I walked in slow contemplation, alone in the wilderness that now reigned over my mind. I paused at the end of the path but did not turn back.

© MR STEGGELS ADVANCED INSTRUCTION PTY LTD

23. At first, the narrator's attitude about actually viewing the canyon can best be described as

    A   reluctant
    B   excited
    C   dread
    D   matter of fact

24. In the second paragraph, the narrator is most concerned

    A   that the weather will turn bad
    B   about finding the best spot from which to view the canyon
    C   that his accommodations are ready and that he won't miss dinner
    D   that the canyon will fail to match his expectations

25. Which sentence best captures the idea that the canyon is overwhelming in scale?

    A   I was filled with equal parts awe and dread.
    B   I struggled to adapt to this new reality.
    C   I looked long into the abyss and tried to understand it in one immeasurable idea.
    D   The huge expanse of time spent gouging, in solid earth, a canyon so immense, crushed all ambition.

26. Choose the best interpretation of the following sentence:

    The mighty scene captured the destiny of all living things.

    A   The canyon made all human ambition meaningless
    B   The canyon would remain when all life on Earth had ceased to exist
    C   The canyon held the secret to the meaning of life
    D   All living things would be captured in the rock as fossils

27. In describing the canyon, the narrator contrasts

    A   his own attitude and the attitudes of the group of observers
    B   the age of the canyon and the short span of his own life
    C   the mass of the everlasting rock and the lightness of cloud vapour
    D   all of the above

© MR STEGGELS ADVANCED INSTRUCTION PTY LTD

28. Which word does not belong in this group of similar words?

   A   pout
   B   smirk
   C   fidget
   D   simper

29. From the following group of letters, remove something to drink and leave something to eat

| C | T | I | O | D | A | E | S | R | T |

How many letters should be removed?

   A   4
   B   5
   C   6
   D   7

30. Sam and Tim are the same height. Combined with their sister Gina, their height is 252cm. Gina plus Sam's is 180cm. What is the difference in height between Gina and Tim?

   A   18cm
   B   36cm
   C   72cm
   D   none of the above

31. I am thinking of a word that when pronounced differently has these two meanings

   (1) to get smaller
   (2) a written agreement signed by all parties involved

These words begin with the letter

   A   r
   B   i
   C   c
   D   a

32. The word **shrewd** is most similar in meaning to

   A   bold
   B   traitorous
   C   small in stature
   D   astute

33. If the day three days after tomorrow is Wednesday, then the day three days before yesterday was

   A   Wednesday
   B   Tuesday
   C   Thursday
   D   Saturday

34. The letters in **lesions** can be rearranged to form a word that means

   A   reduce
   B   classes
   C   feline
   D   alone

35. Which word belongs to this group of similar words?

   banshee   imp   sprite

   A   gypsy
   B   troll
   C   minstrel
   D   urchin

© MR STEGGELS ADVANCED INSTRUCTION PTY LTD

END OF TEST

Test 5

This table is for questions 1—2

City	Annual rainfall (mm)	Maximum temperature in December (°C)	Maximum temperature in August (°C)	Sunshine hours per day
Albertine	994	21.5	13.7	7.2
Berryvale	1451	27.4	16.6	7.6
Carrowdale	698	30.6	16.7	7.9
Felden	1273	22.8	14.0	8.1
Hamilton	762	26.4	15.3	7.6
Madistone	801	31.7	17.9	7.4
Richmond	1325	25.8	15.9	7.3
Yorthe	528	27.9	16.1	6.9

1. The average sunshine hours per day for all cities is

    A   7.8
    B   7.6
    C   7.5
    D   7.4

2. The greatest difference between maximum and minimum temperatures is

    A   11.1
    B   13.8
    C   13.9
    D   14.1

3. Which is **a bird** and also **a chess piece**?

    A   rook
    B   knight
    C   pawn
    D   king

4. In a grade of 64 students, 33 play cricket, 28 play tennis while 10 play not sport. The difference between the number of students who play both cricket and tennis is

    A   7
    B   3
    C   5
    D   none of the above

5. In a bin of mixed fruit, ⅜ are oranges. The rest are apples and pears. There are 350 more apples and pears than oranges. There are four times as many apples as pears. How many more apples are there than pears?

    A   700
    B   525
    C   350
    D   175

6. Water flowed into a 48L tank at a rate of 3L every 15 seconds. At the same time, water flows out of the tank through a tap at the rate of 3L every 10 seconds. If the tank was hall full to begin with, after how many minutes will it be empty?

    A   1min 20sec
    B   8min
    C   6min
    D   4min

7. Someone who begins a lawsuit against another person in a civil court in known as the

    A   lawyer
    B   prosecutor
    C   judge
    D   plaintiff

8. I invested $600 in a bank account that attracted 8% interest, which was added at the end of each year. What was the balance of my account at the end of 2 years?

    A $648.00
    B $688.00
    C $696.00
    D $699.84

© MR STEGGELS ADVANCED INSTRUCTION PTY LTD

Choose the best words to complete the passage

The Rio Grande

The Rio Grande is a major river _____ (9) in southwest United States and northern Mexico. It forms a natural border between Texas and Mexico. It is approximately 870 000 square kilometers (336 000 square miles) in area.

The Rio Grande is either the fourth or fifth longest river system in North America, depending on how it is measured. Because the river twists so much, it occasionally changes _____ (10). These shifts can cause it to be longer or shorter. At its last official measure, the Rio Grande was 3 051km (1,896 miles) in length. It is up to 18m (59ft) deep.

The Rio Grande begins in Colorado and extends downward to the Gulf of Mexico. It is formed by several streams that join at the base of Canby Mountain in the San Juan Mountains, just east of the Continental Divide. It picks up _____ (11) water from the San Juan-Chama Diversion Project from the Rio Chama. A major tributary, the Rio Conchos, enters at Ojinaga, Chihuahua, below El Paso, and supplies most of the water in the border segment. Other tributaries include the Pecos and the Devils, which join the Rio Grande on the site of Amistad Dam.

The Rio Grande flows for most of its length at high elevation through Albuquerque and El Paso. In New Mexico, the river flows through the Rio Grande rift from one basin to another, cutting canyons and also supporting a fragile ecosystem on its flood plain. Downward is the best way of describing its _____ (12). It gets lower and lower in elevation as it extends to the Gulf.

Its name is Spanish for the "Big River," but the Rio Grande is actually known as Rio Bravo in Mexico. "Bravo" translates as "furious". Because of its twists and turns it certainly seems to be more furious than most rivers!

The river ends in a small, sandy delta at the Gulf of Mexico. During parts of 2001 and 2002, the mouth of the Rio Grande was blocked by a sandbar. In 2003, the sandbar was cleared by high river flows and the river once again reached the Gulf.

The Rio Grande cannot be used by ocean-going ships or even smaller passenger boats and cargo barges. It is barely _____ (13) at all, except by small boats in a few places.

9. Choose the most suitable word for position 9

   A   running
   B   beginning
   C   system
   D   ending

10. Choose the most suitable word for position 10

    A   distance
    B   area
    C   length
    D   course

11. Choose the most suitable word for position 11

    A   additional
    B   fresh
    C   treated
    D   less

12. Choose the most suitable word for position 12

    A   progression
    B   position
    C   elevation
    D   none of the above

13. Choose the most suitable word for position 13

    A   recognised
    B   useful
    C   navigable
    D   sailed

© MR STEGGELS ADVANCED INSTRUCTION PTY LTD

14. The **equator** is to **zero latitude** as _____ is to **zero longitude**.

    A   The Tropic of Cancer
    B   The Tropic of Capricorn
    C   Prime meridian
    D   The International Date Line

15. Unscramble these groups of letters and choose the only one that is **not a country**

    A   odbcaami
    B   uyprcs
    C   nmazao
    D   utiawk

16. Sam is ⅕ younger than Frank who is ⅔ younger than Mike who is 3 years younger than Harold who will be 50 in two years. How old is Sam?

    A   8
    B   10
    C   12
    D   24

17. Which is not a meaning of the word **float**?

    A   To be consistent or in keeping with something else
    B   To propose a plan for consideration in order to see what response it receives
    C   Money that has been set aside as change before beginning to sell items at a stall
    D   A truck that has been decorated to take part in a parade

© MR STEGGELS ADVANCED INSTRUCTION PTY LTD

18. Unscramble the following letters and choose which is **a member of the antelope family**

    A   kipoa
    B   zleaegl
    C   leapwof
    D   mlala

19. In a certain code, **duck** is written **bren**. How would **goat** be written in the same code?

    A   fnbv
    B   flbw
    C   elyq
    D   elcw

20. A word can be placed before these words to make new, compound words

    _____visor   _____structure   _____sonic   _____intendent

    This word begins with the letter

    A   u
    B   l
    C   m
    D   s

21. Which idiom has a meaning that is different from the other three?

    A   to cash in one's chips
    B   to checkout
    C   to eat humble pie
    D   to turn up one's toes

22. I have 40% more money than Sam. If I give Sam $120, he will have 40% more money than me. How much money do we have in total?

    A $300
    B $420
    C $620
    D $720

Read the text and answer questions 23—27

Interview conducted by Andrew Thompson BAC Broadcasting Corporation with Underground Economy Taskforce chairman Emily Wales 12/07/2017

Thompson:	Can you give our listeners a bit of an insight into the issue; this so called 'underground economy'?
Wales:	Firstly, tax evasion or participation in a 'black market' or underground economy is illegal. Participants attempt to hide their behaviour from government or regulatory authorities. Violations of the tax code involving income tax evasion constitute membership in the unreported economy.
Thompson:	Just how big is the problem?
Wales:	Because of the clandestine nature of the black economy, it is not possible to determine its size and scope. But estimates have put it as high as $40 billion. That is equivalent to a fleet of 12 new submarines. My job is to advise the Federal Government on how best to tackle the problem.
Thompson:	Has it only recently become widespread or are we just realising the full scope of tax evasion in this country?
Wales:	The extent of non-compliance is, quite frankly, staggering. Particularly in the areas of trades, labour hire, cleaning and courier businesses. It is endemic to every sector. People have become emboldened in recent times.
Thompson:	What will the taskforce target?
Wales:	Our main focus is fraudulent invoicing. The most quoted ABN in Australia is *Tradies Hardware*. Every tradesman goes to *Tradies* to buy their materials. They quote that ABN to customers instead of their own which means that tax authorities can never trace who they are or how much cash they are receiving.
Thompson:	They deliberately conceal their own ABN?
Wales:	If they even have one. Yes.
Thompson:	What other areas are you looking at?
Wales:	We want to remove $100 notes from Australia currency. They facilitate tax evasion. Forty-six precent of our currency is $100 notes. Where are they? Do you see many from day to day? I don't. Criminals thrive on $100 notes. The sharing economy is also a concern—AirBnb, Uber, Airtasker. We have people who really don't understand their tax obligations under these sharing apps. Every time an individual rents a property, drives someone around the city or hires himself or herself out to do a job, they are obligated to pay tax on that income.
Thompson:	There were reports recently on sales suppression software. Can you elaborate?
Wales:	There are accounting systems that obliterate sales records. For example, the software can remove all $10 receipts, or whatever denomination you choose. There is no audit trail. It occurs mainly in the restaurant trade where a lot of cash changes hands. This software is illegal and we are developing detection systems.
Thompson:	What is your message to people who are knowingly participating in the underground economy?
Wales:	I say to them, we know *what* you're doing and *how* you're doing it. It is only a matter of time before we know *who* you are.

23. According to Emily Wales, tradesmen, in particular, avoid paying tax by

    A   deliberately misquoting their ABN when invoicing their clients
    B   pretending that they work for *Tradies Hardware*
    C   hiding their behaviour from regulatory authorities
    D   participating in the sharing economy

24. The interviewer's first question is aimed at providing the listener with

    A   a definition
    B   a recount of important events in detail
    C   an alternative point of view
    D   important background information

25. Which word in the text means **kept secret because forbidden by law**?

    A   clandestine
    B   endemic
    C   fraudulent
    D   evasion

26. Choose the best meaning of the word **facilitate**

    A   prevent
    B   make harder
    C   encourage
    D   compel

27. According to Emily Wales, which method of tax evasion could be due to a lack of education?

    A   fraudulent invoicing
    B   hiding cash reserves in the form of $100 notes
    C   the sharing economy
    D   sales suppression software

© MR STEGGELS ADVANCED INSTRUCTION PTY LTD

28. There are six people in my cannonball team. We need to choose a captain and a vice captain. How many different possibilities are there?

    A   12
    B   30
    C   36
    D   more than 36

29. I read one page of my textbook every Monday, two pages every Tuesday, three pages every Wednesday and so on up to seven pages every Sunday. If I started reading on Monday, on which day would I reach read page 120?

    A   Saturday
    B   Thursday
    C   Wednesday
    D   none of the above

30. Which code should replace the question mark?

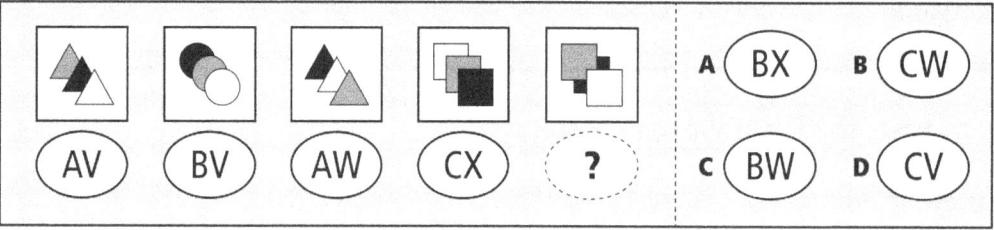

31. Which word does not belong in the same category as **sombrero**?

    A   anorak
    B   fedora
    C   stetson
    D   boater

© MR STEGGELS ADVANCED INSTRUCTION PTY LTD

32. C
33. A
34. A
35. B

Test 1 solutions

Q	A	Explanation
1	B	This is an information report. The first paragraph provides a definition of the subject.
2	C	fortified means strengthened against attack
3	B	attrition is the process of reducing something's strength or effectiveness through sustained attack or pressure → weakening contrition is the state of feeling remorseful / sorry for the bad things you have done
4	A	To the south of the Acropolis was the Theatre of Dionysus.
5	D	A the term acropolis is used to describe many buildings throughout the world (paragraph 2) B Pericles lived in the 5th century (495BC – 425BC). The attack was in 1687. C Restoration work used 2 500 tonnes of original material and 700 original stones D Important and fragile sculptures need to be protected from destruction and pollution
6	A	distend means to swell or cause to swell from inside pressure endear means to cause to be liked or loved
7	D	X = one curly line, Y = 2 curly lines, Z = 3 curly lines S = white circle, T = black circle, U = grey circle
8	C	r = @ a = 4 i = 7 n = L k = Y AKIN = 4Y7L
9	C	Our savings are in the ratio of Sam (2): Jen (6): Me (1) 9 total parts $1890 ÷ 9 = $210 Sam (2 x $210 = $420) : Jen (6 x $210 = $1260) and Me ($210)
10	C	Average sales are indicated by the thick black line. Average sales are dropping back to $36 000, similar to figures in Jan, 2011, which was two years earlier
11	C	The highest actual sales figure is about $40 500 (March 2012 & April 2012). The lowest sales figure is about $35 800 (August 2012 and November 2012) $40 500 - $35 800 = $4700
12	B	I see → I have seen I know → I have known
13	A	This poem is about various spoken vowel sounds
14	A	The poet repeats as in to create rhythm—the beat of the poem
15	D	u☐ as in unite (yoo) as in cute c(yoo)te
16	A	à as in ask (arr) as in c(arr)st
17	B	The poet is mainly interested in spoken sound so this poem is intended to be read aloud.
18	A	The L on the circumference is pointing clockwise in B, C and D, but counter-clockwise on A
19	D	The phrase through thick and thin means to support/stand by someone through good times and bad; through all obstacles and adversity
20	C	The 1st figure is rotated 180° clockwise and appears in the 3rd square The 2nd figure, when rotated 180° clockwise into the 4th square, is C
21	C	¼ + $^2/_5$ + $^1/_{10}$ → $^5/_{20}$ + $^8/_{20}$ + $^2/_{20}$ = $^{15}/_{20}$. So the $^5/_{20}$ or ¼ that is left = 10 hectares If ¼ = 10 hectares, $^4/_4$ = 40 hectares
22	B	silk, wool and cotton are natural fibres; nylon is synthetic
23	B	F = 3 stars, H = 2 stars, G = 1 star L = vertical line, K = horizontal line, M = diagonal lone
24	D	30% of 200 = 60 peaches 70% of 200 = 140 other fruit After some peaches were picked, 80% was other fruit and 20% were peaches. 80% other fruit = 140 and 20% = 35 60 peaches dropped to 35 peaches so 25 were picked.

25	D	Foods, particularly cheese, are referred to as mild in flavour or sharp in flavour
26	A	P is the only letter without vertical symmetry
27	D	A theory is a supposition or a system of ideas intended to explain something, especially one based on general principles independent of the thing to be explained. These words are all synonyms of theory
28	C	day 1 (40°F) + day 2 (54°F) + day 3 (50°F) + day 4 (56°F) + day 5 (59°F) + day 6 (66°F) = 325°F ÷ 6 = 54.14°F
29	A	Pattern: x 2 – 1, x 2 – 2, x 2 – 3, x 2 – 4, x 2 – 5, x 2 – 6 3 x 2 = 6 – 6 = 0
30	C	$57.80 x 8 = $462.40 860 x 15cents = 12900cents = $129.00 $462.40 + $129.00 = $591.40
31	D	A thesaurus contains lists of words with similar meanings.
32	B	5 L takes 20 days to evaporate → 250mL per day (250mL x 20 = 5 000mL) 7 L @ 250 per day will take 28 days to evaporate (250mL x 28 = 7 000mL)
33	A	Travel time = 45mins 45min = 63km (divide both by 9) 5min = 7km (multiply both by 12) 60min = 84km which is 84km/h
34	B	A scarf is worn on the neck; a fez is worn on the head toga a loose flowing outer garment worn by the citizens of ancient Rome fez a flat-topped conical red hat with a black tassel on top camisole a woman's loose-fitting undergarment for the upper body, typically held up by shoulder straps. espadrille a light canvas shoe with a plaited fibre sole.
35	C	The 1st, 3rd and 5th tiles are one pattern. The 2nd and 4th are another pattern. From the 1st to the 3rd, add 2 black squares above the line. The single black square below the line remains unchanged.

Test One score summary															
General ability	Question	6	7	8	12	18	19	20	22	23	25	26	27	31	34	35	Total
	Tick/cross																
Reading	Question	1	2	3	4	5	13	14	15	16	17	Total				
	Tick/cross															
Mathematics	Question	9	10	11	21	24	28	29	30	32	33	Total				
	Tick/cross															

Test 2 solutions

Q	A	Explanation
1	C	Prime numbers between 20 and 50 → 23, 29, 31, 37, 41, 43, 47. Added together = 251
2	A	appease means pacify or placate (someone) by agreeing to their demands
3	D	Coat price: 60% = $312 10% = $52 100% = $520 40% of $520 = $208 $520 + $208 = $728
4	A	48 + 6 = 54 There are 6 parts to the ratio (Tammy had 5 times more than me → 1:5) 54 ÷ 6 = 9 I have 9 marbles and Tammy has 9 x 5 = 45 If I have 9 marbles, I must have started with 9 – 6 = 3
5	C	A glossary of terms is included with an instruction manual as there is usually a substantial amount of technical language. These terms need definitions

6	D	Phase: If two tracks are in sync, they are being played at the same tempo and phase. The beats of both tracks are aligned.
7	D	Musical Instrument Digital Interface—a digital language and hardware specification that allows compatible electronic instruments, sequencers, computers to communicate with each other
8	B	While the terms apply to DJ-ing generally, this information is for DJs who are using digital mixing software. The main clue is that the vinyl control button simulates the sound and feel of vinyl.
9	B	Headphone cueing is listening in your headphones to the next track you would like to mix in. The audience cannot hear what you are cueing in your headphones. This is a crucial aspect to DJing.
10	B	⅔ of the journey = 180km so ⅓ = 90km 90km @60km/h will take 1.5 hours 180km took 3 hours the first 90km took 1.5 hours total travel time = 3 + 1.5 = 4.5 hours
11	B	F = 1 triangle, G = 2 triangles, H = 3 triangles K = black, L = white, M = grey
12	B	foothill: a low hill at the base of a mountain or mountain range. foothold: a place where a person's foot can be lodged to support them securely, especially while climbing. Footnote: an additional piece of information printed at the bottom of a page. Footbridge: a bridge designed to be used by pedestrians.
13	D	freed → defer which means to postpone / put off until a later date
14	D	A Xuds are never red and all Zeds are red → no Zeds are Xuds B All Yips are blue but Woxs are yellow or red → no Yips are Woxs C Zeds are red but no Yips are red → no Zeds are Yips D All Yips are blue and Xuds can be blue → some Yips are Xuds
15	B	cue (a signal to an actor or other performer to enter or to begin their speech or performance) and queue (a waiting line especially of persons or vehicles) are homophones; so are marshal (an officer of the highest rank in the armed forces of some countries) and martial (relating to fighting or war)
16	D	The bicycle stops between 3.5 and 5 seconds; it does not slow down. It does not travel at a constant speed. 45m in 8 seconds 5.625m in 1 second
17	D	77 ÷ 8 = 9 remainder 5 (five left over) 77 ÷ 9 = 8 remainder 5 (four pencils short of 9)
18	C	m = q, a = p, d = b, x = e, n = t mend = qxtb
19	D	A = black vertical line B = two dashes in vertical line C = 4 dashes in vertical line Z = three horizontal lines with arrows Y = three horizontal lines with circles X = three horizontal lines with squares
20	A	$^2/_7$ x 196 = 56 196 – 56 = 140 $^2/_7$ x 140 = 40 140 – 40 = 100 $^2/_5$ x 100 = 40 100 – 40 = 60
21	A	This is a series of prime numbers. The next prime after 11 is 13.
22	B	A kite is not a regular polygon as all of its angles and all of its sides are not equal
23	D	Australia has many tourist spots. Bondi Beach is a favourite destination for many travelers.
24	B	Jane is an anagram of Jean; Arnold is an anagram of Ronald
25	C	$36 is 75% of the original price divide both by 3 → $12 = 25% multiply both by 4 → $48 = 100%
26	D	post = 1234 soap = 3281 tape = 4817 step = 3471 p = 1 o = 2 s = 3 t = 4 a = 8 e = 7 pesto paste = 17342 18347
27	C	The widow's son uses witchcraft (necromancy) to beg the silent spirits to awaken and thereby summon their fugitive sovereign (the king of the dead)
28	C	The poet has used alliteration to build drama. These are long, complex words that do sound like a conjuring spell, but in the repetition of the same sound, suspense and drama are created.

29	C	ghosts are spirits or apparitions
30	A	supplicating means to ask or beg for something humbly the widow's son is begging the spirits to awaken from the dead
31	D	There are many clues in the poem that tell us what necromancy is. The widow's son gives a sermon (or spell) aimed at awakening ghosts, the riggers of death, he is unleashing his blackened heart to cast a fearful curse…
32	C	A: recorder B: trumpet C: triangle D: pentagon
33	D	New kid on the block: one who is new to the group or area Flash in the pan: one who shows potential in the beginning but who fails to deliver in the end Devil's advocate: one who takes a position in an argument without believing in that position
34	B	perch: a place where someone or something rests or sits, especially one that is high or precarious. perch: an edible freshwater fish with a high spiny dorsal fin, dark vertical bars on the body, and orange lower fins.
35	C	The length is 7.5cm and the width is 5.5cm → 7.5 x 2 = 15cm 5.5 x 2 = 11cm 15 + 11 = 26cm 7.5cm x 5.5cm = 41.25cm^2

Test Two score summary																
General ability	Question	2	11	12	13	14	15	18	19	22	23	24	26	32	33	34	Total
	Tick/cross																
Reading	Question	5	6	7	8	9	27	28	29	30	31	Total				
	Tick/cross															
Mathematics	Question	1	3	4	10	16	17	20	21	25	35	Total				
	Tick/cross															

Test 3 solutions

Q	A	Explanation
1	B	1 apple ($2.50) + 1 banana ($1.50) = $4.00 ($2.50 x 8) + ($1.50 x 6) = $20 + $9 = $29 ($2.50 x 6) + ($1.50 x 8) = $15 + $12 = $27
2	B	**avid**: having or showing a keen interest in or enthusiasm for something aware: having knowledge or perception of a situation or fact **eager**: strongly wanting to do or have something apathetic: showing or feeling no interest, enthusiasm, or concern shrewd: having or showing sharp powers of judgement; astute
3	A	The pattern runs down the columns: -2 then +1 column 2: 3, **1**, 2, 0, 1 column 3: 5, 3, **4**, 2, 3
4	B	A cannot be true because Dean did not come 2nd C cannot be true because Dean beat Col in race 2 D cannot be true because Andy finished last in race 2
5	A	There are two patterns: 1st, 3rd, 5th, 7th, 9th, and 2nd, 4th, 6th, 8th, 1st pattern: 1, 3, 6, 10, 15 (+2, +3, +4, +5, +6) next value is 21 2nd pattern: 1, 3, 7, 13, 21 (+2, +4, +6, +8, +10) next value is 31
6	B	Beginning with the circle, the pattern clockwise is: circle, triangle, ring, addition, star, square, heart.
7	A	superlative: of the highest quality or degree ordinary: commonplace or standard

8	C	Abbey and Brian: $330.30 ÷ 6 = $55.05 (subtotal → $110.10) Cathy paid 1/5 more than $55.05 = $55.05 + $11.01 = $66.06 (subtotal → $176.16) Dennis paid 10% of $330.30 = $33.03 (subtotal → $209.19) Enid paid $26 (subtotal → $235.19) Frank paid 1.5 x $26 = $39 (subtotal → $274.19) Gina paid the remainder of the bill = $330.30 - $274.19 = **$56.11**
9	C	meteoric: very rapid. spectacular produced on a large scale and with striking effects. **exemplary**: serving as a desirable model; very good. **consummate**: showing great skill and flair flawed: imperfect impeccable: in accordance with the highest standards; faultless.
10	B	The top curve on the pound symbol (£) points to the curved back of the Euro symbol (€). When the $ sign is folded under, the top curve sits directly under the bottom curve of the € symbol.
11	D	Alphabet shift code | A	B	C	D	**E**	F	G	**H**	**I**	J	K	L	M	N	O	P	Q	R	S	**T**	U	V	**W**	X	Y	Z
---	---	---	---	---	---	---	---	---	---	---	---	---	---	---	---	---	---	---	---	---	---	---	---	---	---
n	o	p	q	**r**	s	t	**u**	**v**	w	x	y	z	a	b	c	d	e	f	**g**	h	i	**j**	k	l	m	
12	C	⅝ = girls ⅜ = women ⅔= boys ⅓ = men ⅓ men = 3 out of 9 This ⅜ for women is equal to the 3 out of 9 for men = 17 total parts (8+9) 289 ÷ 17 = 17 So there are 5 x 17 girls = 85 3 x 17 women = 51 6 x 17 boys = 102 3 x17 men = 51
13	D	All three items feature Bulgarian feta
14	C	Supreme, Napolitana, Capriciossa, Chilli, Pesto, Fresh
15	C	Pepperoni has only two: sliced spicy pepperoni & mozzarella
16	A	large gluten free ½ Garlic Prawn ½ The Sea pizza: $22 + $2 (½ and ½) + $3 (gluten free) = $27 penne arrabiatta = $14, wedges = $9, Greek salad = $10 $27 + $14 + $9 + $10 = $60 Change from $100 = $40
17	C	Mozzarella is used in Margarita, Pepperoni, Garlic, Supreme, Napolitana, Capriciossa, Hawaiian, BBQ meat lover, Chilli, Pesto, Antipasto, BBQ chicken, Peri Peri, Fresh Garlic prawn, Basil and buffalo Mozzarella salad
18	B	Top row: white, black, white, black (circles appear 4 times then disappear) Middle row: white, black, white, black (circles appear 4 times then disappear) Bottom row: white, black, white, black
19	A	Frail (adjective) = weak; robustness (noun) = strength → opposites Longwinded (adjective) = continuing at tedious length; brevity (noun) concise and exact use of words in writing or speech
20	D	0.375 = ⅜ is left ⅝ has been used ⅛ → 1224 ÷ 8 = 153L 153L x 5 = 765L
21	C	Pattern: every 3rd, 5th, 7th, 9th letter → xz **s** bd **e** fg **a** ec **t** ay hg **a** ln **l** tq **p** om **s** ki
22	B	distance covered in 1st 4 hours: 4 x 88 = 352km distance covered in 2nd 5 hours: 5 x 52 = 260km Total distance covered: 352 + 260 = 612km over 9 hours 612 ÷ 9 = 68km/h
23	A	(1) a [narrow] miss is as bad as a wide miss - they are both misses (2) to a person who is ready to understand or undertake something, any subtle signalling of it is sufficient (3) when all is said and done, a thing is what it is (4) to speak plainly - to describe something as it really is
24	B	⅓ is the same as 3 out of 9. I sold 3 out of 9 red marbles and had 6 out of 9 left. One of these sixths is the same as the original number of blue + 20 that I bought. So, out of a total of 720 marbles, nine parts belong to red and one part belongs to blue. That is 10 total parts. Each part is worth 72 marbles. So, there were 72 – 20 blue marbles to begin (52) and 72 x 9 red marbles (648) (648 + 52 = 720) The difference is 648 – 52 = 596
25	B	The child fell through the gap in the floor onto the sand **below**.

26	C	Forensic means the application of scientific methods to the investigation of crime
27	C	Charlie peered at **me** over the top of his handbook. 'You'd better pay attention, **Laura**,' he said.
28	D	We can conclude that Dad said something sarcastic about Nan when she said *I feel like a criminal already*. For example, *That's because you are.*
29	A	Fingerprinting is important in identifying exactly which individual committed a crime because no two sets of fingerprints are ever the same, which means there can be no doubt that a criminal was at a crime scene.
30	D	Laura is suggesting that the forensic kit contains items more suited to a professional than a child.
31	C	96 x 3.5 = 336 The train travelled for 3.5 hours. 9:45am + 3.5 hours = 1:15pm
32	D	**shove** rhymes with **above** hove is the past tense of heave a grove is a small group of trees mauve is a pale purple colour
33	D	lctooe → ocelot
34	D	A: 2 + 3 + 4 + 9 = 18 1 + 8 = 9 B: 1 + 0 + 6 + 5 = 12 1 + 2 = 3 C: 2 + 6 + 4 + 5 = 17 1 + 7 = 8 **D: 8 + 1 + 7 + 3 = 19 1 + 9 = 10 1 + 0 = 1**
35	A	Minimum temps: 13 + 15 + 14 + 13 + 12 + 11 = 78 78°C ÷ 6 = 13°C Maximum temps: 25 + 24 + 26 + 28 + 21 + 14 = 138 138°C ÷ 6 = 23°C 23°C − 13°C = 10°C

Test Three score summary															
General ability	Question	2	4	6	7	9	10	11	18	19	21	23	25	32	33	34	Total
	Tick/cross																
Reading	Question	13	14	15	16	17	26	27	28	29	30	Total				
	Tick/cross															
Mathematics	Question	1	3	5	8	12	20	22	24	31	35	Total				
	Tick/cross															

Test 4 solutions

Q	A	Explanation
1	C	According to Pythagoras' theorem, where a is the perpendicular height of the triangle, b is the base and c is the hypotenuse: $a^2 + b^2 = c^2$ → $a^2 + 6^2 = 10^2$ → $a^2 + 36 = 100$ $a^2 = 64$ a = 8
2	B	Volume of cube = 6 x 6 x 6 = 216cm³ Volume of hole = 3 x 3 x 6 = 54cm³ It isn't 3 x 3 x 3 because the hole must go right through the 6cm cube. 216 cm³ − 54 cm³ = 162 cm³
3	A	raccoon → corona
4	D	A: robin B: swift C: eagle D: shark
5	D	Add the letter m to champion
6	D	The letters in the first column are in their normal alphabetical orientation

7	B	$984 \div 2 = 493$ $1 + 492 + 493 = 986$ $493 \div 2 = 264.5$ $1 + 246 + 247 + 492 = 986$
8	B	Risen to recur → resurrection
9	C	Patients with port-wine stains may need 6-10 treatments. Patients with facial redness and blood vessels will usually require 2-3 treatments.
10	D	Side effects: red, and swollen skin, some lightening or darkening of the skin, thinning of the skin and scarring.
11	C	The skin may also be firmer and tighter due to the stimulation of new collagen production.
12	B	treatment and procedure are used throughout the text and mean the same thing—using the Perfecta Laser on the patient's skin.
13	C	Exercise increases blood flow to the skin, which will increase redness.
14	A	The pattern is +1, +2, +3, +4, +5 … Signs appear at 1, 2, 4, 7, 11, 16, 22, 29, 37, 46, 56, 67, 79, 92, 106, 121, 137, 154, 172, 191, 211
15	B	The code is skip 2 letters back, then jump 2 letters forward K l m, i j K, V w x, e f G, B c d N o p, l m N, Y z a, n o P, R s t
16	A	infamy: the state of being well known for some bad quality or deed. disrepute: the state of being held in low esteem by the public.
17	D	The sides of the tank are 10m. Half filled with water, the level is 5m. The volume of the concrete block: 10m x 10m x 1.25m = 125m³ The water level will rise by 1.25m. The new height will be 5m + 1.25m = 6.25m
18	B	Southern ocean → Coral sea
19	C	Rolling three fives is 1 possibility. There are 6 x 6 x 6 possibilities with three six-sided dice, which is 216. The chances are 1 out of 216
20	C	sulk: be silent, morose, and bad-tempered out of annoyance or disappointment. soak: to wet thoroughly bawl: weep or cry noisily. brood: think deeply about something that makes one unhappy, angry, or worried. fret: be constantly or visibly anxious.
21	A	Left hemisphere → 26 + 22 + 45 + 7 = 100 Right hemisphere → 13 + 70 + 3 + 14 = 100
22	C	0.75kg for $1.35 multiply by 8 → 6kg for $10.80 0.5kg for $0.90 multiply by 12 → 6kg for $10.80 1.5kg for $2.60 multiply by 4 → 6kg for $10.40 2.0kg for $3.50 multiply by 3 → 6kg for $10.50
23	A	The narrator is loathe (reluctant) to exchange his hopes about the canyon for memories of it. Once he has seen it, it will then only be a memory.
24	D	The canyon is finally within reach and the narrator is anxious about being disappointed.
25	C	I looked long into the abyss (canyon) and tried to understand it in one immeasurable idea. The canyon is so vast that it is unable to be measured.
26	B	The canyon would remain when all life on Earth had ceased to exist—the destiny of all living things is, finally, death. The canyon is everlasting and, therefore, captures human existence in its timescale.
27	D	A unaffected by the magnificent panorama, rather deep and worth looking at B vastness of the canyon crippled all human accomplishment C I was merely a transient, no more than vapour rising into thin air above everlasting rock.

28	C	pout: push one's lips or one's bottom lip forward as an expression of petulant annoyance smirk: smile in an irritatingly smug, conceited, or silly way. fidget: to make small movements, especially of the hands and feet, through nervousness or impatience. simper: smile in an affectedly coquettish, coy, or ingratiating manner.
29	B	Remove C I D E R (something to drink) to leave T O A S T (something to eat)
30	B	G + S = 180cm G + S + T = 252cm therefore 180cm + T = 252cm T = 72cm If T = 72cm then S = 72cm G = 180 – 72 = 108cm G – T = 108 – 72 = 36cm
31	C	contract means to get smaller A contract is a written agreement signed by all parties involved
32	D	shrewd: having sharp powers of judgement bold: showing a willingness to take risks traitorous: disloyal, unfaithful small in stature: small in size astute: clever, sharp-witted
33	B	If three days after tomorrow is Wednesday, tomorrow is Sunday and today is Saturday. Yesterday was Friday and three days before that was Tuesday.
34	C	lesions → lioness = feline (cat)
35	B	banshee: (in Irish legend) a female spirit whose wailing warns of a death in a house. imp: a small, mischievous devil sprite: an elf or fairy. gypsy: a member of a travelling people traditionally living by itinerant trade and fortune telling. troll: (in folklore) an ugly cave-dwelling creature depicted as either a giant or a dwarf. minstrel: a medieval singer or musician, especially one who sang for the nobility. urchin: a young child who is poorly or raggedly dressed.

Test Four score summary																
General ability	Question	3	4	5	6	8	15	16	18	20	28	29	31	32	34	35	Total
	Tick/cross																
Reading	Question	9	10	11	12	13	23	24	25	26	27	Total				
	Tick/cross															
Mathematics	Question	1	2	7	14	17	19	21	22	30	33	Total				
	Tick/cross															

Test 5 solutions

Q	A	Explanation
1	C	7.2 + 7.6 + 7.9 + 8.1 + 7.6 + 7.4 + 7.3 + 6.9 = 60 60 ÷ 8 = 7.5
2	C	Albertine 21.5 – 13.7 = 7.8 Berryvale 27.4 – 16.6 = 10.8 Carrowdale 30.6 – 16.7 = 13.9 Felden 22.8 – 14 = 8.8 Hamilton 26.4 – 15.3 = 11.1 Madistone 31.7 – 17.9 = 13.8 Richmond 25.8 – 15.9 = 9.9 Yorthe 27.9 – 16.1 = 11.8
3	A	rook: a chess piece, typically with its top in the shape of a battlement rook: a crow with black plumage and a bare face, nesting in colonies in treetop
4	C	64 – 10 = 54 (the number of students who do participate). There are 33 + 28 = 61 who play cricket and tennis. There are 61 – 54 students who play both = 7 Cricket → 33 – 7 = 26 Tennis → 28 – 7 = 21 The difference is 26 – 21 = 5
5	B	⅜ are oranges ⅝ are apples and pears Difference between the two 5 – 3 = 2 shares = 350 1 share = 175 5 x 175 are apples and pears = 875 There are 4 times as many apples than pears which is 5 total shares 875 ÷ 5 = 175 apples = 4 x 175 = 700 pears = 1 x 175 700 – 175 = 525
6	D	Water flows in at 6L every 30 seconds and flows out at 9L every 30 seconds. It loses 3L every 30 seconds. The tank is half full. 3L x 8 = 24L 30sec x 8 = 240sec = 4min
7	D	lawyer: a person who practises law, especially a solicitor or a barrister or an attorney. prosecutor: a barrister who conducts the case against a defendant in a criminal court. judge: a public officer appointed to decide cases in a law court. plaintiff: a person who brings a case against another in a court of law.
8	D	In the first year, 8% of $600 is added to the account, which is $48 ($^{8}/_{100}$ x 600) The new balance is $648. In the second year, another 8% of $648 is added, which is $51.48 ($^{8}/_{100}$ x 648) The balance at the end of two years is $648 + $51.48 = $699.84
9	C	The Rio Grande is a major river system in southwest United States and northern Mexico.
10	D	Because the river twists so much, it occasionally changes course. These shifts can cause it to be longer or shorter.
11	A	It picks up additional water from the San Juan-Chama Diversion Project from the Rio Chama.
12	A	Downward is the best way of describing its progression.
13	C	It is barely navigable at all, except by small boats in a few places. Navigable means able to be sailed on by ships or boats.
14	C	The equator constitutes the parallel of latitude 0°. Prime meridian is the zero line of longitude
15	C	A: Cambodia B: Cyprus C: Amazon D: Kuwait
16	C	Harold is 50 – 2 = 48. Mike is 48 – 3 = 45. Frank is ⅓ of Mike's age (⅔ younger) = 15 Sam is ⅘ of Mike's age (⅕ younger) = 12
17	A	float does not mean to be consistent or in keeping with something else
18	B	The okapi and the giraffe are the only living members of the family Giraffidae. A gazelle is any of many antelope species in the genus Gazella The peafowl include three species of birds in the genera *Pavo* and *Afropavo* of the pheasant family The llama is a domesticated South American camelid

19	D	Pattern: 1st letter skip back 2. 2nd letter skip back 3. 3rd letter skip forward 2. 4th letter skip forward 3.
20	D	supervisor superstructure supersonic superintendent
21	C	A, B and D all mean to die. To eat humble pie is to make a humble apology and accept humiliation.
22	D	Sam has 140% to my 100% = 240% 40% = $120 so 240% = $120 x 6 = $720
23	A	Tradesmen are using the ABN that belongs to *Tradies Hardware* on their invoices to clients, instead of their own, which means that they have lied in order to not pay tax on that income.
24	D	The interviewer's question gets a response from the interviewee in which she defines what a black market or underground economy is, but the question asks for background information.
25	A	clandestine: kept secret because it is illegal endemic: widespread fraudulent: involving deception evasion: avoiding something—in this case, paying tax
26	C	$100 notes facilitate tax evasion—they make it easier to avoid paying tax → encourage
27	C	We have people who really don't understand their tax obligations under these sharing apps
28	B	There are 6 potential captains, each with 5 potential vice captains e.g. 1 with 2, 3, 4, 5, or 6 6 x 5 = 30
29	B	Each week I read 1 + 2 + 3 + 4 + 5 + 6 + 7 pages = 28 Each Sunday I will end on a multiple of 28: 28, 56, 84, 112 Mon = page 113, Tues = pp114-115, Wed = pp116-118, Thurs = pp 119-122
30	D	A = triangles, B = circles, C = squares V = white at front W = grey at front X = black at front
31	A	sombrero a broad-brimmed felt or straw hat worn in Mexico and the south-western US. anorak: a waterproof jacket, typically with a hood, of a kind originally used in polar regions. fedora: a low, soft felt hat with a curled brim and the crown creased lengthways. stetson: a hat with a high crown and a very wide brim, worn by cowboys in the US boater: a flat-topped hardened straw hat with a brim.
32	C	To evaporate liquid some form of heat is needed.
33	A	1st pattern: Z y X wv U T s R pq O N m L kj I 2nd pattern: A b C de F G h I jk L
34	A	Warm voice → microwave
35	B	This proverb means *a little precaution before a crisis occurs is preferable to a lot of fixing up afterward.* A better to be happy with what you have than to risk losing everything by seeking to get more. B if you sort out a problem immediately it may save extra work later. C a person who has injured another person is to be penalised to a similar degree D If a group's members are in perpetual disagreement, the group will eventually cease to exist.

Test Five score summary

	Question	3	7	14	15	17	18	19	20	21	30	31	32	33	34	35	Total
General ability	Tick/cross																
Reading	Question	9	10	11	12	13	23	24	25	26	27	Total					
	Tick/cross																
Mathematics	Question	1	2	4	5	6	8	16	22	28	29	Total					
	Tick/cross																

www.ingramcontent.com/pod-product-compliance
Lightning Source LLC
LaVergne TN
LVHW061316060426
835507LV00019B/2182